HOLIER
THAN THOU

CONSTANTINE GREY

ISBN: 978-1-967375-36-3 (Paperback)
ISBN: 978-1-967375-37-0 (E-book)

Library of Congress Control Number: 2025913832

Printed in the United States of America

Published by:

info@thequippyquill.com
(302) 295-2278

HOLIER

THAN THOU

TABLE OF

CONTENTS

PROLOGUE

Much has been written and debated about the impact on society of the negative aspects of religion in recent years, and by people slightly more erudite and articulate than myself. However, I still sense that a calm, objective debate about the strengths and weaknesses of religion must continue until such time that concrete steps are taken to correct the immoral teachings of the scriptures.

What fuels me is mainly the religiously stimulated murder and terrorism of this current era and the threat it poses to worldwide peace. If nuclear weapons get into the equation, our very existence is threatened. At the head of a long list, the frustration and irritation I feel when watching supposedly learned pro-religion apologetics and official representatives of religion selling or debating their side with arguments of pure casuistry and dishonesty. Also, watching some televangelists spewing their nonsense with frequent selective references to the scriptures to enthuse and sometimes fleece the vulnerable flock while skillfully avoiding mention of the evil-causing parts of the texts.

For this study, the position taken by theists that there was a divine intervention is set aside, and an attempt is made to delve into the evidential roots of the so-called monotheistic religions of Christianity, Islam, and Judaism. The objective is to try to arrive at a better understanding of how and why they were created based on facts as opposed to reported relationships with the supernatural.

The final objective is to strengthen the platform for debate and ultimately to help stimulate a self-induced catharsis of those negative parts of the gospels that provide the framework for each religion. The literal translation of the Torah, Bible, and Qur'an is perceived by most non-theists as the root of many of the ideological problems in the World today.

There appears to be a generally accepted view relative to the historical creation and evolution of religion that ignorance of the realities of science was the main causative factor. There is a belief that the ancients created responses based on the supernatural to explain destructive weather, geological anomalies such as eruptions, planetary movement, disease, plagues, and the moral and social interplay between one human being and another. This could be true in many cases.

However, there is firm evidence to indicate that not all ancients were in awe of nature in that manner and that some had a surprising grip on reality to the point that they did not accept the ethereal rationalization of the storytellers.

In terms of recorded history and as early as 1600 BCE which was well before the promulgation of the Abrahamic holy texts, skeptics and critics made themselves known and their observations were aptly recorded. There is strong reason to believe that even well before this time and as early as those eras when certain dogmas were being concocted and passed on to others, there existed non-believers and they were, ironically, among religion's creators. The numerous references in the holy texts to non-believers indicate that there were many and, because of the negative and derisive manner in which they have been referred indicate that they posed a threat to the ideology that was being proposed.

In the earliest recorded history, it is evident that religion became a tool of ruling bodies once it was realized what power it wielded over the masses. Unbelievers closeted their skepticism for fear of severe punishment or even death or they assumed the position of a follower but utilized the belief system to better their lot in life or to maintain control of those beneath them as what could have been the case with many priests.

The fact that early Christian Church leaders protected the belief system with harsh reprisal against non- believers including, in many cases death for heretics, is a strong indication it had to be protected or they ran the risk of losing it to the people who were capable of employing sensible logic. This was one of the main implements that kept them in an elevated position.

Even today, the hierarchy in certain Islamic states deals very seriously with perpetrators accused of heresy, blasphemy, or apostasy. The Qur'an and Hadith state that an apostate should be executed.

Priestly types and religious leaders have always had a revered and elevated social status in all civilizations. This condition persists even in modern-day societies and political structures. Ordinary people who have become clerics are revered and are held in high esteem and bowed to by devout followers simply based on the religious title that they hold.

Along with the general critique of the Abrahamic religions, the book takes a side trip to a beautiful island in the Aegean called Santorini, where a monstrous explosion occurred 3600 years ago and was probably the cause of the Great Flood as described in the Bible.

Further discussion is concentrated on the World crime rate as it relates to the religiosity of people, with surprising results plus a study of the business side of religious institutions, past and present.

An additional review involves the afterlife, its effect and whether or not it really exists.

When we cut through all the rituals, ceremony, mysticism and the supernatural, we find that religion is basically one small group of people trying to tell a very much larger group of people how to behave.

I
CONDITIONS
PRECEDENT

In order to attempt to offer my view regarding the circumstances and players involved in the establishment of the main Messianic religions, Judaism, Christianity, and Islam, I believe it would be of value to briefly review the history and background of those humans responsible for promulgating their own particular theistic belief system.

Science has proven that modern human beings or Homo sapiens evolved in Africa from a group of apelike creatures over a period of approximately four million years. Of course, this somewhat contradicts the story given in the Bible about the creation.

Through fossil records, paleoanthropologists have determined that Homo sapiens or basically modern man first appeared on the scene about 200,000 years ago in the mid to eastern part of what is now Africa.

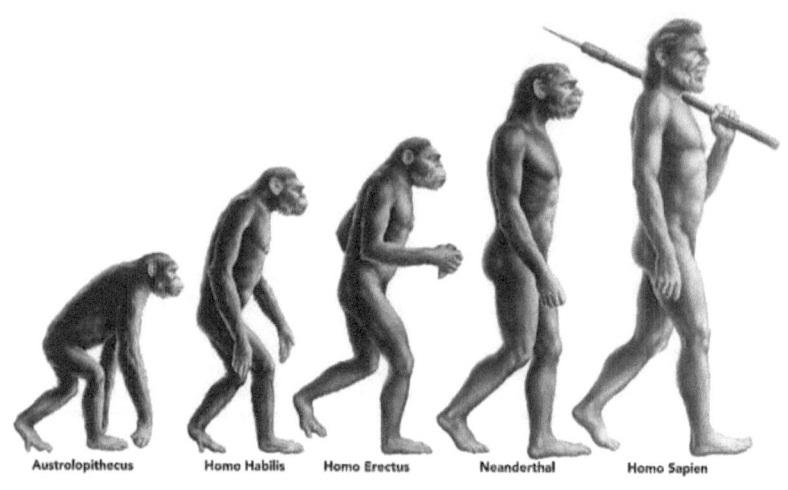

Austrolopithecus   Homo Habilis   Homo Erectus   Neanderthal   Homo Sapien

About 70,000 years ago, these same Homo sapiens began a migration out of Africa through the Middle East and then spread into the vast Eurasian land mass and further to Australasia. As part of their expansion that also took them into what is now Europe, the Homo sapiens encountered the lesser developed Neanderthals and may have been responsible for their extinction while taking part of the time of their excursion to partially interbreed. The ancestors of Neanderthal man were of the same genetic source as Homo sapiens but previously had exited Africa at the Homo erectus stage of development about 630,000 years earlier.

It should be noted that Homo sapiens then bore the same cranium size as modern man. Even the Neanderthals, who have been improperly demeaned as being slow were actually quite clever and had a cranium capacity even greater than that of Homo sapiens.

Exodus of Homo Sapiens from Africa

As an aside and given the fact that present-day humans, whether brown, black, or white, all emanated from Africa, an intriguing and ironic anomaly is created. Does this mean that the White Supremacists in the United States must consider themselves African Americans? It appears so.

These modern humans continued their lives as hunter-gatherers until about 12,000 years ago when a momentous transition started. It marked the introduction of agriculture as the mainstay for life support as the Neolithic Revolution exploded onto the scene! The evolution from bands of hunter-gatherers to an agro-based society resulted in the most rapid and dramatic leap forward in the advancement of cultured civilization.

The Neolithic Revolution, which is also known as the Agricultural Revolution, worldwide took two or three millennia to take effect. It marked a major turn for modern humans who began cultivating their land for crops and retaining livestock to supply meat and dairy products. It was to change their whole style of living and would cause populations to grow significantly and rapidly as they became less migratory. It also would allow them the time to think of things other than their survival.

With this transformation came a more complicated and structured life. Before, as hunter-gatherers, humans lived in small bands of ten to twelve adults plus offspring. What they called home was inclined not to be permanent, as they followed migrating herds or moved to seasonally richer territories in order to properly feed themselves. Interaction among individuals in the band has been deemed to have been egalitarian, with perhaps an alpha male as the tribal leader.

This was to change with the new agricultural system, as defined land became a valuable asset. Simplistically speaking, this raised many basic questions among the populace, the main issues being: Who owned the land? Who owned the livestock? Who supplied the product and labor to cultivate the land and maintain the livestock? And, to whom were the final products to be distributed, and for what remuneration?

In other words, while a promising new form of civilization had developed with the advent of the Neolithic, the resulting interpersonal and intertribal competition and chaos brought out the best and the worst in humans but eventually gave cause for the establishment of an economic system and a means of being governed. It then followed a system of law and order in which we may include religion. This process did not happen immediately and required centuries to coalesce and usually involved strife and, many times, physical battle between disagreeing factions. It also marked the birth of royal dynasties as the more powerful clans and individuals took control.

Ultimately, a two-class society developed with the establishment of an authority structure separated from the common people. The authority structure became the elite and usually evolved into some sort of kingship.

The Neolithic gave rise to the need for a system of accounting and recording. This meant that whatever language was being spoken by the new civilizations, by necessity, had to be visually codified and documented. With the establishment of alphabets to describe the phonetics being used to verbally communicate, writing evolved, first in Sumer, Mesopotamia around 3500BCE. A whole new era was born, and it is here too, that formalized religion was able to take root.

Cuneiform Writing from Mesopotamia circa 3500BCE

Since agriculture requires fresh water for its daily maintenance and long-term survival, the Neolithic Revolution took place, for the most part, in four major watershed systems in Asia and Africa.

- In East Asia, the Yellow River

- In mid-Asia, the Indus River

- In Mesopotamia, the Tigris and Euphrates Rivers

- In Africa, the Nile River

The last two on the list were located in the Fertile Crescent. The lands and cities located therein, including Egypt, Palestine, Israel, Judea, Phoenicia, Assyria,

Babylon, Ur and Sumer, were to play an important role in the establishment and history of God-type religions and eventually, Judaism, Christianity and Islam.

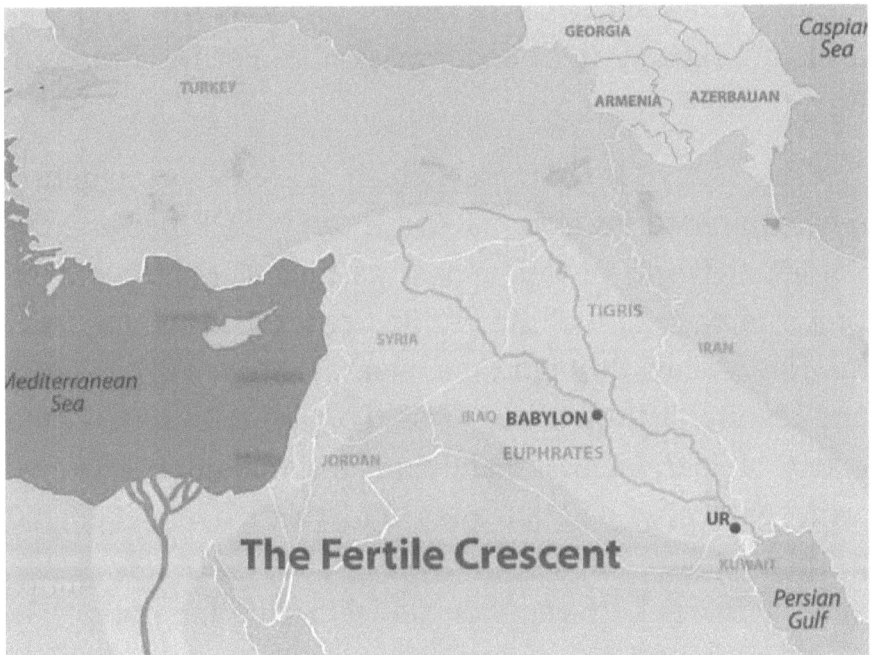

With the system of writing originating in the Sumerian culture in the form of cuneiform lettering, it became possible to codify the beliefs into literally hard copies on clay tablets.

The profession of scribe evolved and became an elite position within the social structure of the Mesopotamian states.

This is an attempt to try to capture the frame of mind of the authority structure and people of pre-Judaism, Christianity, and Islam. A pertinent study in this regard revolves around the Assyrian, Babylonian, and Persian

Empires. The first two originated in upper Mesopotamia and have been referred to many times in the Bible while Persia evolved geographically from the area to the east of Mesopotamia and what is known today as Iran and was to later expand and encompass the Fertile Crescent, Egypt, and Turkey.

The Assyrian Empire which lasted a staggering nineteen centuries from 2500BCE to 609BCE became the dominant world power and at its height, controlled the vast trading region of the Fertile Crescent stretching from the Nile Valley, through the Levant, Eastern Turkey, Iran, and ending at the Persian Gulf. To give relevance to the extent of its domain, it maintained a standing professional army of almost 400,000 men and ruled over 4,000,000 people. Rulers of this empire made themselves the intermediaries between their subjects and their gods.

It is in Assyria where the mythological foundation of the old and new testament is found. It is here that the story of a great flood originates, 1000 years before the Old Testament is written. It is here that the first classic is written, the 'Epic of Gilgamesh', with its universal and timeless theme of the struggle and purpose of humanity. It is here that civilization itself is developed and handed down to future generations. It is here where the first steps in the cultural unification of the Middle East are taken by bringing under Assyrian rule the diverse groups in the area.

Finally, it is here that the Assyrians established, after many centuries, the modus operandi for controlling a large, well-spread population utilizing a strong army and a system of sacred beliefs that relied heavily on the supernatural, both of which ultimately affected a respect by the populace for their power and authority.

From Iran to Egypt, ethnic and national barriers were broken down, which prepared the way for the cultural unification and facilitated the subsequent spread of Hellenism, Judaism, Christianity, and Islam.

Priests held a very high position in the Assyrian social structure in the same strata as the wealthy and just below royalty. It is clear that they were not appointed by the establishment but earned their status because of the perceived immense power they wielded. It is here, around 2,000 BCE, that we identify the application of 'priestcraft' on a large scale. Priests in most religions carry a high degree of power. This was quite evident in the early days of the Catholic Church and with today's Islam, where the perceived act of heresy was and is still being treated severely.

In order to ensure and protect their elevated status and the privileges that went with it, the priesthood took the traditional beliefs that prevailed and moulded them into a form of religion that required strict adherence and reverence to the kingly leaders of the empire. This also solidified their position within the power structure.

While the Assyrian religion in play from 1600BCE to about 200CE was described as polytheistic, it would be more accurate to describe it as henotheistic. This type of belief system requires a supreme deity, which in the Assyrians' case, they called Ashur, while recognizing the existence of many other lesser deities.

Theistic religions, such as those followed by Fertile Crescent occupants, were formulated by leaders of the state who propagated ancient lore into an organized belief system to suit themselves and their people.

Religions spawned in the Fertile Crescent during the Bronze Age all carried a similar cast of characters, but some with different names.

CHRONOLOGY OF MAJOR RELIGIONS

	Age in Years	Adherents
Hinduism	4,000	1.1 billion
Judaism	3,800	15 million
Shinto	3,000	5 million
Buddhism	2,500	506 million
Confucianism	2,500	6 million
Taoism	2,300	12 million
Christianity	2,000	2.4 billion
Islam	1,400	1.9 billion

It should be noted that Christianity and Islam with the highest membership of all major religions are the newest belief forms. Not included in the above list is the Secular category at about 1.2 billion which is comprised of the nonreligious, agnostics, and atheists.

Homo sapiens have existed for 200,000 years yet it took 196,000 years before a religion was formally created. Clearly, it was the Neolithic Revolution starting 12,000 years ago that created the need for structured systems of belief that would assist in maintaining law and order in the social chaos that ensued.

Christianity presents itself as a monotheistic religion yet it recognizes the presence of Satan who is effectively a god, although an adversarial one. It appears that the principal God is powerless against him. This religion also accepts the existence of angels who are supernatural beings that purportedly act as intermediaries between humans and God. Islam also believes in Satan along with mini-gods known as Jinn who are supernatural creations that are believed by the followers to influence human life.

In going through a cerebral exercise of how, hypothetically, I would establish a new religion, I imagined encountering a number of hurdles that I would have to clear. As an example, this new religion would be based solely on the Golden Rule: 'Do unto others as you would have them do unto you.' The first question from my potential followers would probably be; Who am I to preach to them or tell them what to do? Shunning the logical answer that it was the right thing to do because they still might not follow me, I would suggest that it is coming from a mysterious higher source who inspired me and is telling me what to do. Their next question is; Well, who or what is this mysterious source? My answer; Well, it happened like this… (use your imagination and fill in the blank).

It also gave me a better understanding of how the many different religions might have been created.

II
THE LEGITIMACY OF THE MESSIANIC RELIGIONS

DO THE CRIMINAL CONTENTS IN THE HOLY TEXTS DENY THEIR USERS THE ABILITY TO FUNCTION LEGALLY UNDER WESTERN LAW?

There has been much written and debated about the negative content in the Bible and the Qur'an. I am taking it a step further and saying that it breaks Western criminal law.

The written doctrines of the Messianic religions contain death threats to legally innocent individuals thereby contravening secular criminal law. Further, there are many examples of statements made, particularly in the Qur'an that incite hatred against nonbelievers of Islam. Many detractors have criticized religion but, to date, there has been little commentary on the criminality of those parts of the scriptures that break the law.

The carrying out of literal instructions from the holy books of Islam and Christianity has been responsible for wars and serious crimes against humanity in the past two millennia, and it continues to this day.

WHAT DOES THE LAW SAY?

This brings up the question: Do the death threats and inflammatory rhetoric in the messianic scriptures break the law in the functioning of their related religions?

To cite a case in point, the following are excerpts from Canadian Federal Criminal Law, which provide a credible example of how most Western democracies legally deal with common death threats. The UK goes a step further in making the maximum term for imprisonment ten years. The essential words have been underlined to emphasize that not only uttering a death threat but also conveying or causing a person to receive such a threat carries the same punishment.

CONVEYING DEATH THREATS

264.1. Uttering threats

264.1 (1) Everyone commits an offence who, in any manner, knowingly utters, conveys, or causes any person to receive a threat

(a) to cause death or bodily harm to any person; ... (Punishment)...

(2) Every one who commits an offence under paragraph (1)(a) is guilty of:

(a) an indictable offence and liable to imprisonment for a term not exceeding five years; or

(b) an offence punishable on summary conviction and liable to imprisonment for a term not exceeding eighteen months.

Further, Western democracies also deal with the incitement of hatred against any particular identifiable group and treat it as a crime. Again, using the Canadian model, this is how it is stated.

WILFUL PROMOTION OF HATRED

> *319(2) Everyone who, by communicating statements, other than in private conversation, willfully promotes hatred against any identifiable group is guilty of:*
>
> *(a) an indictable offence and is liable to imprisonment for a term not exceeding two years; or*
>
> *(b) an offense punishable by summary conviction.*

WHAT DO THE SCRIPTURES SAY?

It is well-known that the scriptures of Messianic religions, along with many positive sentiments, house a substantial number of violent and immoral edicts that reflect threats to the well-being or life of many categories of people. Some apologists for their religion tend to explain them as having been written in a metaphorical or allegorical style and not to be taken literally. However, there have been a multitude of cases where certain religiously devout followers have applied the literal interpretation with lethal results.

With respect to Islam, certainly anyone who wishes to leave the religion as an apostate or, in fact, need only be what the scriptures describe as an infidel or nonbeliever should have cause to feel threatened for his life by those who have declared openly that they follow the literal dictates of Islamic writings. Any member of the religion who publicly declares himself or herself a literalist believer, of which there appears to be a majority of Muslims, by definition, could pose a threat. However, we know that common sense usually prevails and abuse is not rampant, but the feeling is with many people outside the religion that on coming into contact with a person of the Islamic faith, one never knows for sure what his or her sentiments. While not excusing Christianity and Judaism, especially for the past atrocious crimes related to the Church, the greatest concern today for those desiring world peace is what is being and could be done by Islamic "radicals". It is within the Hadith of this relatively new religion that appear statements and references that categorically state that a believer who leaves the Muslim faith should be killed.

Hadith Bukhari 9.84.57 *"Whoever changed his Islamic religion, then kill him."*

To give some substantiation to this claim from Muslims themselves, it has been documented that there is a consensus among the four schools of Sunni Islamic jurisprudence (Maliki, Hanafi, Hanbali, and Shafii) as well as classical Shiite jurists that those who leave the faith of Islam must be put to death. One can only guess at how many Muslims exist today who wish to leave their faith but are fearful for their lives if they were to do so. The number could be substantial.

Over and above the threat to apostates, both the Qur'an and the Hadith contain inflammatory pronouncements concerning the marginalization and even the killing of unbelievers of Islam.

There are over one hundred verses in the Qur'an that call Muslims to war with unbelievers for the sake of Islamic rule, effectively attempting to incite hatred by Muslims of this rather large group. Some are quite graphic with commands to chop off heads and fingers and kill infidels wherever they may be found. Those of the faith who do not join the battle are labeled as 'hypocrites' and warned that Allah will ban them to Hell if they do not join the battle.

Here are some examples:

> Qur'an (5:33) *"The punishment of those who wage war against Allah and His messenger and strive to make mischief in the land is only this, that they should be murdered or crucified or their hands and their feet should be cut off on opposite sides or they should be imprisoned; this shall be as a disgrace for them in this world, and in the hereafter they shall have a grievous chastisement"*

> Qur'an (8:12) *"I will cast terror into the hearts of those who disbelieve. Therefore, strike off their heads and strike off every fingertip of them."*

Qur'an (9:5) *"So when the sacred months have passed away, then slay the idolaters wherever you find them, and take them captive and besiege them and lie in wait for them in every ambush, then if they repent and keep up prayer and pay the poor-rate, leave their way free to them."*

Qur'an (9:73) *"O Prophet! strive hard against the unbelievers and the hypocrites and be unyielding to them, and their abode is hell, and evil is the destination."*

Qur'an (9:123) *"O you who believe! fight those of the unbelievers who are near to you and let them find in you hardness (ruthlessness)."*

Qur'an (17:16) *"And when We wish to destroy a town, We send Our commandment to the people of it who lead easy lives, but they transgress therein; thus the word proves true against it, so We destroy it with utter destruction."*

Qur'an (48:29) *"Muhammad is the messenger of Allah. And those with him are hard (ruthless) against the disbelievers and merciful among themselves"*

These are but a few of the hundred-plus recommendations for the severe treatment of nonbelievers of Islam.

Purely and simply, the holy Islamic writings reflect proclamations that are illegal, and immoral and ultimately have had and continue to have a negative effect on society and, in certain cases, threaten world peace. They convey unequivocal recommendations to their readers to murder people under certain conditions while concurrently condoning and even encouraging human slavery, both of which are clearly illegal under Western criminal law.

While Islamic extremists are presently at work playing havoc with the world, Christianity has also had its run on the stage of religious fanaticism.

The following are just some quotations from the Bible where it is clearly decreed that people be put to death for religiously perceived infractions.

Kill People Who Don't Listen to Priests

> *Anyone arrogant enough to reject the verdict of the judge or of the priest who represents the LORD your God must be put to death. Such evil must be purged from Israel. (Deuteronomy 17:12 NLT)*

Kill Witches.

> *You should not let a sorceress live. (Exodus 22:17 NAB)*

Kill Homosexuals

"If a man lies with a male as with a woman, both of them shall be put to death for their abominable deed; they have forfeited their lives." (Leviticus 20:13 NAB)

Kill Fortune tellers

A man or a woman who acts as a medium or fortune teller shall be put to death by stoning; they have no one but themselves to blame for their death. (Leviticus 20:27 NAB)

Death for Hitting Dad or Mom

Whoever strikes his father or mother shall be put to death. (Exodus 21:15

Death for Cursing Parents

1) *If one curses his father or mother, his lamp will go out at the coming of darkness. (Proverbs 20:20 NAB)*

2) *All who curse their father or mother must be put to death. They are guilty of a capital offence. (Leviticus 20:9 NLT)*

Death for Adultery

If a man commits adultery with another man's wife, both the man and the woman must be put to death. (Leviticus 20:10 NLT)

These decrees have been basically ignored in the modern era because there are secular laws to protect society, and the Church is not as powerful as it used to be in influencing these laws.

HISTORICAL TRANSGRESSIONS BY LITERAL FOLLOWERS OF THE SCRIPTURES

In the past, probably the most abused of the edicts of the Bible has been the directive to kill witches. The infamous Christian-backed witch hunts took place between the years 1450 to 1800. Estimates by social scientists indicate that the murdering of innocent females referred to as witches mostly by being burnt alive in Europe and North America exceeded some 250,000 women. The number may be debatable but the fact is not.

The biblical pronouncement evolved into secular law and was applied against women who were deemed to be involved in sorcery. It should be recognized that the punishment of sorcerers and sorceresses historically has not been confined only to Christian countries and has taken place in other cultures, however at not anywhere near the same intensity and level.

The tragic irony of this horrifying piece of history is that most people today deny the existence of witches and sorcerers.

Islam also has a past. The Armenian Christian genocide at the hands of the Islamic Ottoman Turks started in 1915 and, perhaps fueled by the strong anti-infidel tonality in the scriptures of the Qur'an, resulted in the massacre of an estimated 1,500,000 Armenians.

However, the fact still remains that there are evil and immoral proclamations and threats of death in the so-called Holy Scriptures which are followed literally by many people that have been the source of social upheaval and serious crimes against humanity. They continue to be a source of problems even today.

These have to be corrected if the human factions on this earth are to begin to successfully evolve into a mature and peaceful world-wide society. There are many of us who believe that a major step towards neutralizing religious fervour and zealousness would be to defuse some of the damaging rhetoric contained in the scriptures.

While these evil edicts of Judaism and Christianity are ostensibly being ignored by almost all the followers today, a greater concern exists in how the literal interpretation of the Qur'an and Hadith of Islam are being applied by the more radical element of whom there appears to be many.

A revealing study made in 2013 indicates that a majority of Muslims living in Europe would prefer to live under Sharia or the Law as decreed and administered by

Islamic theocracies. This conclusion was drawn in a study published by Dr. Ruud Koopmans from the WZB Berlin Social Science Centre. Data was analyzed from a representative survey among immigrants and natives in six European countries. Two-thirds of the Muslims interviewed said that religious rules were more important to them than the laws of the country in which they lived. Three quarters of the respondents held the opinion that there is only one legitimate interpretation of the Qur'an.

Startlingly, these are European Muslims whom one would think would be more moderate than others of the Islamic faith. If correct however, this would mean that there are theoretically hundreds of millions of Muslims who could be on the brink of becoming radical and who believe in the Allah-given immutability of their religious texts. Of course, being radical does not necessarily mean that one would be willing to commit murder but it could mean that she or he condones those who might do so in the name of Islam.

In recent years, whenever a serious act of terrorism involving death has occurred, it is reported to have been performed by "radicalized" individuals and in almost all cases, people of the Muslim faith. The term "radicalized" is used to describe an apparent metamorphosis that takes place with certain individuals who have succumbed to the sway of others who have a deep-rooted literal view of their religion and this is what makes them commit horrific crimes. The term has been bandied about in the press as if it is a relatively common occurrence, and anyone may be vulnerable. It is apparent that any declared literalist is basically on the brink of being radical and may only need a little shove.

Add this condition to one who is disgruntled with how he or she is being treated by the non-Muslim society in which he or she lives such as that which may be found living in Europe and North America coupled with a firm belief that he or she will be going to a better world upon his or her death and you have someone who is primed to turn radical and cause serious damage. There appear to be more than a few in this category.

Regarding the epidemic of murderous terrorist attacks instigated and performed almost totally by Muslims, particularly in the last two decades, most politicians and justice authorities appear reluctant to criticize Islam as a whole while attributing the attacks to radicalized extremist Islamists. The fear that their own religion or that of a large voting bloc will come under the same criticism may be a causative factor.

The Bible, particularly the Old Testament and the Torah do breaks Western democracy criminal law in that they clearly convey death threats and cause people to receive them. Why there have been no charges laid or, at least, have become a topic of contention with authorities lies in the fact that, in most instances, religion gets a pass.

Politicians and the justice systems of many Western democratic countries appear reluctant to tackle such a sensitive issue, which could result in major societal upheaval while besmirching the name and essence of what is perceived by a substantial portion of the voters and citizens as hallowed and untouchable institutions.

Most media are reluctant to suggest that religion may be the culprit. Being politically correct is to ignore the proverbial eight-hundred-pound gorilla in the room. Reporting after the November 2015 Paris attacks by ISIS-fuelled religious zealots on a concert hall, stadium, restaurant, and bars leaving 130 dead and hundreds wounded, CNN's Christiane Amanpour, a well-respected and knowledgeable international news correspondent, reported on television and suggested categorically that it wasn't religion that was behind the motive to carry out such butchery but, in fact, the desire for totalitarianism by a power group. There are many who think she got it only partially correct.

It is true that most religions, as they have evolved and are practiced, may not be at fault. However, fundamentalist religion or literalist interpretation of the scriptures is responsible, as are the founding documents.

The US President, Barack Obama, and now Donald Trump have stated that their country intends to see to the defeat and stamping out of ISIS. Given the number of fundamentalists who are already on the brink of being radicals from whom ISIS may be able to draw, this may be an almost impossible task.

Most fundamentalists believe that the doctrines arising from the scriptures that form the basis for their religion are as dictated by God. This could somehow be, however, the holy books of the Messianic religions are rife with inflammatory rhetoric and edicts to commit murder and do not appear to be the product of a peace-loving God.

The Messianic religions offer many positives to their followers, including conscience cleansing, forgiveness of sins, a feeling of redemption or salvation, peace of mind knowing that a supernatural force is looking after them, and having someone to talk to when they are alone and perhaps troubled. Further, they offer the possibility of an afterlife in paradise.

Probably at the top of the list for many, they offer a cultural tradition and focal point around which believers may coordinate their moral, social, and family life. However, history has proven that these religions were promulgated mainly by the ruling elite in eras that were emerging from the late primitive stages of societal development and that they reflect many of the socially acceptable practices of the time.

This brings us back to the legality of the holy texts. Why there have been no charges laid or, at least, have become a topic of contention with authorities lies with the fact that politicians and law enforcement agencies do not want to tackle such a sensitive issue which could result in a major societal upheaval while besmirching the name and essence of what is perceived by a substantial portion of the voters/citizens as hallowed and untouchable institutions.

If a decision were to be made to pursue prosecution under the law, a problem would then arise in deciding who might be charged. Certainly, fundamentalists, both clerics and congregation, who publicly espouse the literal veracity of the scriptures, must head the list of those being deemed guilty of agreeing with the content of those texts that contain death threats and promote hatred of others. There are many of the faithful who do not treat the gospels as metaphors and conduct their life based on literal beliefs of the scriptures. In the United States alone, there is an estimate that Evangelical Christians make up over 30% of the population, or about 100,000 million people, representing a huge voting bloc.

WHY MAKE AN ISSUE OF IT?

There have been many cases, even in recent history, where zealots have committed crimes based on their literal interpretations of the directions dictated by the Torah, Bible, and Qur'an and the older historical monstrous abuses, such as burning people alive following the direction of canonical writings were even more widespread and brutal.

After centuries of use and abuse of what are actually, ironically, unholy preachments, a majority of followers of Christianity, if one may generalize and speak for its many sects, have now settled into a compromise situation with reality and have evolved tempered extremist views even if many of the faithful are literalist in their belief.

WHAT ABOUT SLAVERY?

Except for murder, the practice of slavery is next on the list of the most immoral and illegal acts. Yet slavery is rampant throughout the Bible in both the Old and New Testaments. The Bible clearly condones slavery in many passages, and it goes so far as to tell how to obtain slaves, how hard you can beat them (as long as you don't kill them during the thrashing, it's OK), and when you can have sex with the female slaves

Beyond the legal interpretation of the scriptures, rests the moral aspect. Slavery which is against the law in all Western democracies is not only condoned but also recommended in the scriptures of all three messianic religions.

However, slavery being illegal does not mean that there is a crime committed in condoning slavery. It means that a purported enslaved person is not by law a slave, and has all the rights of ordinary people. It follows that anyone trying to enslave them is subject to the normal criminal law (e.g., kidnapping and assault) and the normal civil law (e.g., employment law).

Many Jews and Christians try to ignore the moral problems of slavery by saying that these slaves were actually servants or indentured servants. Some translations of the Bible use the word "servant" or "bondservant" instead of "slave" to soften the tone and make the Bible seem less immoral than it really is. While many slaves may have worked as household servants, that doesn't mean that they were not slaves who were bought, sold, and treated like livestock. It is quite simple. These were the rules of war at the time and taking slaves was a part of sharing the spoils. Bible composers and scribes had no compunction in sanctioning same.

With regard to Islam, slavery is clearly condoned in the Qur'an and many Muslims believe that this book is the literal word of God which cannot be questioned even though social values and respect for human rights have changed dramatically from the days when it was written.

There are many references to slavery in the Qur'an. Some authors describe this as Mohammed's attitude toward slavery. However, many Muslims disagree. To Muslims, Mohammed was God's messenger and Islam's prophet. More correctly, the Qur'anic verses to many Muslims provide a statement of their God's views on slavery. The clear conclusion from all these passages is that the people who wrote the Qur'an and Hadith saw slavery as a natural aspect of human relations and presented it as if it was the will of their God.

TREATMENT OF NON-BELIEVERS and
IMPLIED HATRED IN THE SCRIPTURES
INCITING TERRORISM

The denigration and abuse of non-believing minorities ran its course within the Christian church in the past and appears to be now, out of necessity and sanity, neutral, even though the inflammatory passages remain in the scriptures. However, it appears to be Islam's turn now to take the readings of their holy book to their literal nadir and play havoc with world peace. Clearly, it is a minority who is responding to the recommended extreme treatment of infidels as decreed in the Qur'an. However, the fact remains that the holy book of Islam is rife with belittlement of unbelievers (pejoratively referred to as infidels, dhimmi or kafirs) and is readily open to such interpretation. It would not be unreasonable to suspect that a few of the Muslim clerics are also quietly behind the fuelling of such hatred.

With the Shiite Muslim theocracy of Iran on the verge of obtaining nuclear weapons according to some pundits and ISIS in the process of attempting to form a new territory/country, the threat to world peace continues and certainly, countries like Israel whose very existence is in jeopardy based on documented threats emitted by Iranian leaders.

WHAT TO DO?

It is time that leaders of the respective religions of Judaism, Christianity, and Islam step to the forefront and officially recognize the imperfections in their respective scriptures. Measures must be taken to make amends for the injury they have caused in the past and to dilute the acrimony and potential harm they will continue to cause. This is a moral obligation.

Every time a Pastor, Evangelist, Rabbi, or Imam, in giving a sermon, quotes from their holy book without qualification, he or she are effectively condoning the rest of the contents in that book.

Ideally, the scriptures should be edited to exclude the harmful text. Rewriting them is next to impossible, particularly with Islam and the cast-in-stone irrevocable nature of the Qur'an. However, there could be addenda created to the main scriptures without changing the originals. This would be, at least, a start.

COULD A HOLY CODICIL BE A SOLUTION?

Western common law has a facility for changing a person's Last Will and Testament by allowing the testator to create a document known as a 'codicil' which contains subsequent legally valid, overriding changes to the substance of the Will but leaves the original document physically intact.

Since religions are not restricted by borders, this may well be a task for the United Nations to pursue. This would certainly be a highly contentious and volatile issue, but it is one that should be taken.

It is time that we all grow up and recognize our defects and how they threaten the stability of the world. It is time that we put religion into its proper perspective, that we respect its place in our cultures, but correct the mistakes of the past by redacting the holy texts to rid them of deadly inflammatory rhetoric.

The scriptures should be corrected so that no human life is threatened, that slavery is condemned, and that they reflect civilized moral standards.

The mere act of restating the cancerous scriptures does not mean that such restatement will be adhered to by all, but it is at least a start and a necessary and most important prerequisite to arriving at a more lasting peace.

Until the Torah, Bible, Qur'an, plus Hadith are amended so as to meet legal and moral standards, the synagogues, churches, and mosques and the clerics who run them cannot claim legitimacy in the Western world.

III
MESSAGES FROM
MESOPOTAMIA

When it comes to explaining how the many forms of religion came about, many atheists and even notably respectable and erudite ones such as the late Christopher Hitchens have referred to the fact that the various strains evolved during the early stages of man's development when man was ignorant of science and biology and blamed anomalous physical occurrences on the supernatural. This is one issue wherein I am not entirely in agreement with the late Mr. Hitchens, even though he is a man I greatly admire, both past and present.

In discussing his book, "God Is Not Great: How Religion Poisons Everything," before a large group as a part of the Authors@Google series in August of 2007, Hitchens made the following excerpted comments on the origin of religion: "It is derived from the childhood of our species, from the bawling, fearful period of infancy. It comes from a time that we did not know that we lived on an orb. We thought we lived on a disc... we didn't know there was a germ theory to explain disease, and innumerable theories for the explanation of things like famine. ..."

There is strong evidence indicating that members of the elite of most post-Neolithic societies and especially those whose ethos and religions were to serve as the foundation for today's Abrahamic faiths, Judaism, Christianity and Islam were philosophically and culturally more advanced than has been credited by most historians. This also serves to buttress the theory that some religions were created not just by believers of superstition and the supernatural but by those who may, themselves, have been logical thinking non-theists.

MARI—THE KINGDOM THAT LASTED TWELVE CENTURIES

An important discovery in 1936 by the French archaeologist, Andre Parrot, in the ruins of the King's palace in the City State of Mari which revealed many intimate insights into the everyday life of that era. Mari was an ancient Semitic city located on the much-traveled upper Euphrates River in Mesopotamia in what is today Syria. It flourished as a trade centre and hegemonic state for almost twelve centuries between 2900 BCE and 1759 BCE, many centuries before the creation of the Messianic religions.

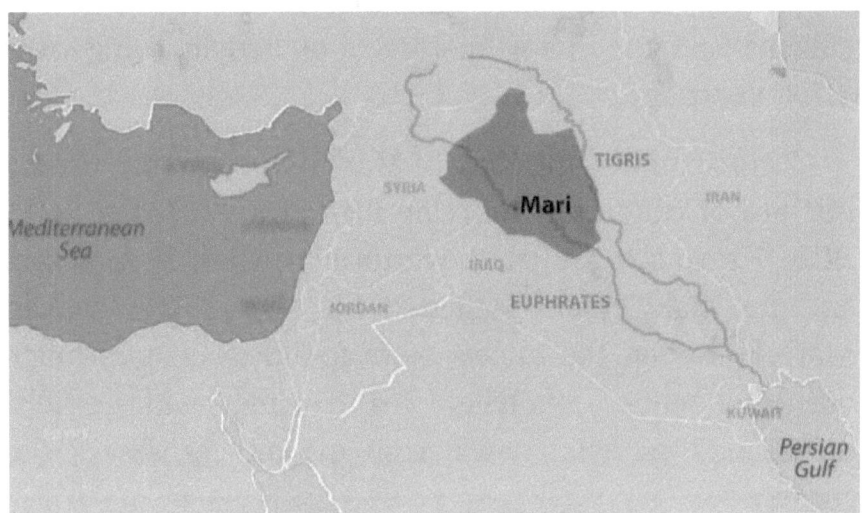

Some 25,000 cuneiform tablets, so numerous that many still await decipherment, were uncovered dating back to from 1800 BCE to 170 BCE. They were later proven to describe in detail essentials from the everyday life of the society of the time.

The contents of the tablets strongly confirmed that members of the authority structure of Mesopotamian society at that time were culturally well developed and far from primitive in their thoughts. They include legal documents and edicts, diplomatic dispatches, reports from provincial officials, medical teachings, records of commercial transactions, school primers for the training of scribes, handbooks for the interpretation of omens and the performance of magical rites, retelling of ancient myths and epics, collections of proverbs, and maxims for readers seeking moral guidance. The tablets have revealed a wealth of information and have given a good insight into the lives and personalities of both ordinary citizens and the ruling hierarchy of people living over 3,700 years ago.

Zimri-Lim was the King of Mari for a brief span during this era of cuneiform scripting from about 1775 to 1761 BCE. He was to be later overthrown when Hammurabi and the Babylonians defeated his armies and sacked Mari. However, the tablets were found to contain much correspondence involving his regime with official documents carrying news from distant corners of the realm.

Some tablets included orders for the construction of canals and dams. One shows a decree for a census of nomads. Another encourages Zimri-Lim to discipline a group of army draftees by having the head of a troublemaker removed. The royal scribes kept lists of over 2,000 local craftsmen, ranked by name and specialty, and even kept a strict accounting of food brought into the palace.

More importantly and relevant to this chapter, there were also numerous documents of a personal nature which offer an insight as to what went on in the minds of the ruling elite within the confines of the palace.

The most significant finding is how Zimri-Lim reveals an understanding of infection and the need to isolate a sick person. In a letter to his wife, he cautions her to take steps necessary to prevent the spread of a very "contagious disease". Zimri-Lim tells his wife to; "Give strict orders. No one is to drink from the cup she uses; No one is to sit on the seat she takes; No one is to lie on the bed she uses for fear that it will infect the many women who are with her". Elsewhere in the royal correspondence, the Queen shows similar concern for her husband in sending him warm clothing in preparation for an excursion while advising him to bundle up so that he doesn't catch a cold.

This should be treated as startling news as we are talking about a point in time that took place over 3,700 years ago and many centuries before the establishment of the Messianic religions. This was supposedly a period in man's development where disease was thought to have been caused by evil spirits or God's punishment for bad behavior. Instead we have a person of significant status, an absolute ruler, apparently aware of the existence of microbes or what most of us know today. One reasonably has to presume that this was not an isolated case and that, as a minimum, his family, members of his court, the priesthood and the ruling elite along with scribes carried similar knowledge.

The microscope was not invented for another 2,100 years so it is not as though Zimri-Lim knew precisely the nature of the microbes but it is apparent that he was aware of their existence. Clearly, the observations made over the centuries of conditions precedent to the occurrence of various illnesses had been noted, possibly documented but in any event, passed on by word of mouth to the subsequent generations.

It should be noted that a not dissimilar occurrence took place when Greek philosopher Democritus around 400 BCE came up with the theory that all matter was made up of microscopic, indestructible tiny particles known as atoms. This was 2,200 years before English chemist John Dalton's development of an atomic theory in 1803. This further exemplifies the fact that among humans at that time, there were very intelligent specimens who were capable of thinking logically, their mind unclouded by the supposed existence of a never-to-be-seen supernatural world.

Fertile Crescent religions were henotheistic and all sported pantheons in varying degree and assortment with one main deity at the head supported by a cast of assistant gods. As a comparison to similar cultures on a contiguous continental landmass, the Chinese, who at that time vastly outnumbered the Egyptians and Mesopotamians in the Crescent, elected to go with ideological belief systems that did not require a principal supernatural deity.

On the mainland of the Far East, religion never became a state administered institution as was the case with the theocracies of the Fertile Crescent where kings and priests either took on or were given the image of being full or partial gods and religious rites were created and supervised by the governing body.

From this writer's perspective, bringing China into the religion creation equation is significant. At the time of the Fertile Crescent empires, China had a population of over thirty million predominantly non-theists while those under the theocracies of Mesopotamia and the rest of the Fertile Crescent including Egypt totalled some four million, all of which were theocracies. I believe that theists might be asking themselves why their particular God selected their little slice of humanity while ignoring a much larger concentration of advanced and cultured Homo sapiens.

This might lead one to suspect that Fertile Crescent religions were the creations of the authority structures at a very early stage of historical evolution and were based on established local lore. What the individual states called their principal gods varied with each particular culture further indicating that no one from up above had taken the time to communicate to and inform them as to his proper name.

This is further evidence to support the theory that the originators of the theistic religions did so out of expedience and practicality perhaps not having the requirement to have even been devout believers themselves.

Declaring human beings as gods was originally arbitrary out of a perceived need by those in power to have the leader place himself or members of the elite including priests in a stratum well above the more or less credulous common people. The most logical reason would have been to concretize the authority structure so as to remain in power with the least possibility of being overthrown.

Historians who make reference to the nature of a belief system that existed at the time for a particular nation might be advised that it would be more accurate to say that these people were ostensibly ordered or perhaps obliquely persuaded to believe in their gods by the authority structure.

A BRIEF WORD ON EGYPT

Probably the most notable member of the Fertile Crescent outside of Mesopotamia is Egypt. With its ancient history well-defined and recognizable by its imposing Pyramids, it remains a prime example of how ancient societies evolved and behaved in the era after the onset of the Neolithic Revolution and before the emergence of the Messianic religions.

The rich Nile Valley produced a wealth of agricultural treasures and eventually gave rise to a very populous and prosperous society.

However, egalitarianism when assets are involved appears not to be a part of the human psyche. Over the centuries and after much strife, an elite class emerged and a kingdom was formed.

In Egypt, the king was known as Pharaoh. To the ancient Egyptians, the Pharaoh was a godlike being, closely identified with their all powerful God Horus. How he was able to attain such a status while still physically remaining a human being has not been documented and, therefore, is open to debate.

Historically kingships in earlier times evolved usually as a result of battle where territory was won or successfully defended and the winning leader was revered and elevated by the fighting minions. Dynasties ensued, their length depending mainly on the quality and strength of the progeny. It is probable that, after many generations of being told you are a god that many Pharaohs, perhaps through delusion, believed they themselves were gods. Hence, the emergence of the great Pyramids and the mummification upon death.

Neighboring Mesopotamia at the other end of the Fertile Crescent experienced a similar process with its kingships.

THE EPIC OF GILGAMESH

Gilgamesh was believed to have been an early king of Uruk in southern Mesopotamia around the year 2700 BCE. In the year 1933 CE, anthropologists discovered numerous tablets written in cuneiform and describing King Gilgamesh and his exploits. The content of these tablets became the basis for the epic poem about a fabulous king and is known as the Epic of Gilgamesh.

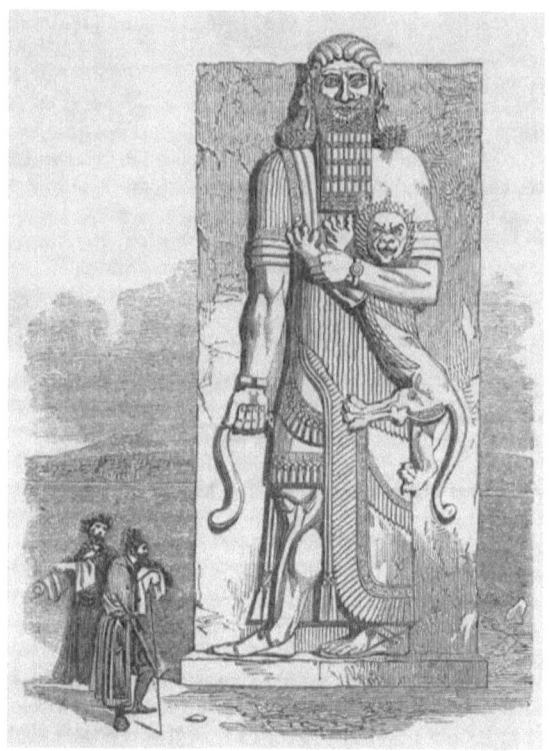

Artist's portrayal of King Gilgamesh

Briefly, he was depicted as the son of King Lugalbanda and the goddess Ninsun, thereby making him a demigod. His height was listed at 5.5 meters or 18 feet. (Others say he was only 9 feet tall.)

In his adventures, he befriends a very unrefined fellow named Enkidu (also very tall) and encounters Utnapishtim, the survivor of a great flood. As one of their most critical exploits, Gilgamesh and Enkidu meet and slay the monster, Humbaba, who was responsible for many evils, including fire, flood, and pestilence.

Gilgamesh later runs into Ishtar, the goddess of love, who is very taken by his persona and asks him to be her consort. He rejects her offer, and Ishtar, very offended, sends down the Bull of Heaven to do him in.

However, Gilgamesh and Enkidu proceed to kill the Bull. For this sacrilege of slaying a deity, Ishtar makes Enkidu pay with his life. Gilgamesh returns to his home in Uruk, now a wiser and more moderate ruler, and builds a magnificent wall to protect its inhabitants during his benevolent rule.

The Epic of Gilgamesh was considered in ancient times to be a masterpiece of Cuneiform literature. Tablets containing parts of the story have been found in Turkey, Syria and Israel after having been originally compiled in Mesopotamia. It was composed at a time when only 10 percent of the population was able to read or write yet it did receive wide distribution with references attested in Greek and Roman literature.

The most complete compilation of the Epic came from a scribe by the name of Sin-leqi-innini, who put together a full set of the twelve tablets covering the entire saga. This was accomplished somewhere between the years 1300 BCE and 1000 BCE.

In summary, it was evidence of how easy was the occurrence and interrelationship between gods and privileged humans and how the Epic might have set the stage for theistic religions to come hundreds of years later.

THE SUMERIAN KING LIST

Although all leaders of societies in their cultural infancy have dabbled with various forms of deification, the first documentary evidence in history of an interplay between a monarch and a supernatural god was unearthed in Mesopotamia in the ruins of the site of ancient Nippur by German-American scholar Hermann Hilprecht (1859-1925). It is known as the Sumerian King List (the List), a 4,000-year-old ancient Bronze Age manuscript written in Cuneiform on clay tablets in the Sumerian language and first made public to the modern world in 1906.

Its author or authors are unknown, but were people of great imagination and intent.

The Sumerian King List

The clay manuscript was written on a rectangular cube form and stands about one meter high. It catalogues a record of the kings of Sumer and neighboring dynasties covering a period of many millennia. The lengths of reign and lifespan of individual monarchs are extremely exaggerated, the early ones in the tens of thousands of years. However, the kings and their period of reign in the latter part of the List are traceable in history, giving it a strong, if not partial, degree of historical credibility. It appears to have been an attempt to link actual historical kings of the era when the List was written with partially or totally fictional godly predecessors, presumably so that they and their progeny would take on the same aura of godliness.

Sumer is relevant to the Messianic religions in that one of its major population centres was the city of Ur, which was the home of Abraham and also Noah, two of the major players in the stories of Judaism, Christianity, and Islam. The List was compiled around 2000 BCE, and the writing of the Torah/Bible began 600 years later, around 1400 BCE, and would be completed over the next 1500 years. To date, there have been eighteen exemplars of the List recovered, each one slightly different in context, attesting to the fact that it was recopied by hand a number of times, probably well circulated among the ruling elite and most likely well known to the erudite Mesopotamian hierarchies of that period.

The List begins with the very origin of kingship, which is seen as a divine institution by the ruling elite. The rulers in the earliest dynasties are represented as reigning for enormously long periods.

It reports that in Eridug, Alulim became king; he ruled for 28,800 years. Alaljar ruled for 36,000 years. Two kings, who ruled for a total of 64,800 years.

Some of the rulers mentioned in the early part of the List include Lugalbanda and Gilgamesh of the renowned Epic of Gilgamesh, described earlier in this chapter.

The List names eight kings with a total of 241,200 years from the time when kingship "descended from heaven" to the time when "the Flood" swept over the land and once more "the kingship was lowered from heaven" after the Flood.

Curiously, there are those, today, who believe that there is a basis for reality in the numbers and that the early kings were in fact gods who were capable of living beyond normal human capacity. Again, this shows the power of theistic religions to instill blind acceptance of supernatural tales and stifle man's ability to think coherently.

Any theories that indicate that the regal longevities are true are easily disproved by scientific fact. Archaeologists claim with substantial evidence that Homo sapiens emigrated from Africa to the Eurasian landmass only 70,000 years ago. The only humans occupying Mesopotamia before Homo sapiens arrived would have been Neanderthals. The early kings on the List would have had to have been Neanderthals. This is unfeasible as it has been proven that Neanderthals travelled about as primitive hunter-gatherers in small bands and had not advanced to the stage of having developed large kingship societies. Neanderthals disappeared from the face of the earth about 40,000 years ago, most likely at the hand of the Homo sapiens.

For that matter too, Homo sapiens did not evolve from the huntergatherer stage until the Neolithic Revolution some 10,000 to 12,000 years ago further bringing in to question any validity to the long life spans of the Kings as indicated in the List not that this fact should be a surprise to anyone.

Those kings and their period of reign in the latter part of the List are traceable in history, giving it a strong if not partial, degree of historical credibility. It appears to be an attempt to link actual historical kings from the era when the List was written with partially or totally fictional godly predecessors, presumably so that they and their progeny would take on and maintain the same aura of godliness.

The List is generally regarded as still a mystery to some historians after more than a century of research. However, there is an obvious explanation that must be considered. As kingship became the established method of rule in the various domains of the Fertile Crescent, the need to maintain hegemony, which is historically the prime concern of any regime was determined to be better facilitated by linking monarchs to the supernatural. A deified monarch was more easily respected and feared by the mass majority, which made political power easier and army troop obedience and loyalty more controllable.

The List appears to be hard evidence that the author or authors wanted to present the premise and aura that the ancient fantasy kings and their progeny were deemed to be sent by God and lived for very long periods. It also has a place in history as the first example of religious beliefs being used as a political tool and the official beginning of the game of charades played by the actual kings in Mesopotamia.

The following are quotations by Aristotle and Seneca that might apply to what is being discussed here:

> *A tyrant must put on the appearance of uncommon devotion to religion. Subjects are less apprehensive of illegal treatment from a ruler whom they consider god- fearing and pious. On the other hand, they do less easily move against him, believing that he has the gods on his side.*
>
> *—Aristotle, Politics.*
>
> *Religion is regarded by the common people as true, by the wise as false, and by rulers as useful.*
>
> *—Lucius Annaeus Seneca*

I have observed that historians, when describing a certain religion tend to present it as if it has evolved naturally over time and that it was broadly accepted by the populace. There is very little dwelling on the strong possibility that formal religion was more a product of the elite playing to the masses in order to institute a system of law and order based on the current morals of the time and further, to facilitate their political control. Given all the different names used to describe the supreme deity is adequate proof that he did not take the time to notify people what his name was and that he or she was humanly contrived.

It appears that there is an inner desire in almost everyone to believe in the supernatural and spiritual world. I believe that those in power and the intellectual elite figured this out and used it to their advantage.

It seems reasonable to conclude that the idea that religions were formed out of ignorance and credulity is highly questionable. The Bronze Age (3300 BCE to 300 BCE) world of the Mediterranean, Near East and Middle East was intertwined with many countries and cultures including Greece, Phoenicia, Syria, Mesopotamia and as far east as Afghanistan as trading partners dealing in commodities such as copper, tin, amber, glass and spices. Not only were commodities traded, but also ideas.

At the elite level, society was, for the most part, quite well informed as to how other societies behaved and believed. All this was in practice centuries before the formation of the Messianic religions.

IV
THE GREAT
FLOOD OF THE
BIBLE

WAS IT THE BIG GENIE OR JUST SANTORINI?

The Great Crater of Santorini

In the year 1646 BCE, an island in the central part of the Aegean Sea known then as Thera and now, Santorini, exploded with a force one hundred times that of the devastating Mount Vesuvius eruption that took place in the year 79 CE. Equally dramatic was the fact that the blast was six times larger than the behemothic explosion of the Indonesian island of Krakatoa in 1883 CE. The Santorini upheaval wreaked havoc throughout the Mediterranean while seriously affecting weather patterns encompassing the entire world for many years.

This chapter explores in more detail later on, the theory that this cataclysmic event was the cause of the Great Flood as described in Genesis in the Bible. Most of us are aware of the story of the Great Flood as related in the Torah, Bible and Qur'an.

The Bible's version of the Flood has God, being so dissatisfied with mankind and apparently most of the animals in the world that he decided to destroy them all save a good fellow named Noah, his family and a menagerie of various animals. Excerpt from Genesis:

> *Now the flood was on the earth forty days. The waters increased and lifted up the ark and it rose high above the earth. The waters prevailed and greatly increased on the earth and the ark moved about on the surface of the waters. And the waters prevailed exceedingly on the earth, and all the high hills under the whole heaven were covered. The waters prevailed fifteen cubits (6.9 meters or about 23 feet) upward and the mountains were covered.*

The Bible puts forth the observation that the whole world was inundated and even the mountains were covered with water. There is strong evidence to show that this can be logically disproved and that the flood did not encompass the whole world. After forty days the rain stopped. Later, Noah was reported to have landed his ark atop Mount Ararat in the Atlas Mountains in eastern Turkey. The altitude of Mount Ararat is just under 17,000 feet or 5,200 meters. This would mean that the sea level would have had to have risen over three miles or almost five kilometers. This, obviously, is an impossible feat.

The recorded world record for rainfall in one day occurred in 1952 CE on Reunion Island just east of Madagascar and totaled six feet. If this rainfall rate is applied to Ararat's elevation, not just based on the occurrence on a little island in the Indian Ocean but on a much larger, but unfeasible global basis, it would have taken 2,800 days or almost eight years to reach Ararat's peak.

However, if there is any veracity to the Biblical forty-day and forty nights rain period, then a catastrophic flood could and probably did occur, however, not worldwide. The assumption is that it was the Santorini explosion that caused the flood which therefore restricted its geographical impact to points immediately due east, namely: the Aegean Sea, Turkey, and the Tigris-Euphrates ecosystem.

There is no question that a major flood did occur and it may have sparked the Bible writers to revive and update an earlier report. In fact, flooding in that part of the world and specifically Mesopotamia was not a rarity. Archaeological digs have found that the mud- brick protective walls surrounding cities such as Ur (the one-time home of Noah and Abraham) in the lower part of Mesopotamia where the flooding mostly took place, had been covered with a thick layer of bitumen to protect against erosion caused by the flooding of the Tigris-Euphrates River system. This might explain the earlier version of a flood as it appeared in another notable historic writing, the Epic of Gilgamesh.

Noah and the Great Flood is a newer version of that appearing in an historic publication written in cuneiform known as the Epic of Gilgamesh and whose emergence has been traced back to 2000 BCE. In it, the god Era warns Utnapishtim to build a boat and save his family due to the oncoming rain and inundation. He cautioned that the gods were angry at mankind and wanted to punish them.

There are those of us who believe that what was referred to as the World at the time by those writing the Bible was both the Near and Middle East but mainly Mesopotamia, the home of advanced cultures and also Noah and Abraham. It is probably safe to say that the authors of the Old Testament had not wandered outside of the Near and Middle East and it was the only world they knew.

Abraham is perceived as having been the founding father of the three great monotheistic religions, Judaism,

Christianity and Islam. Noah of Genesis was reported to have captained the Ark and along with his family were supposed to have been the sole survivors of the Flood in the entire world. People living in Mesopotamia at that time utilized boats to navigate the rivers and conduct trade so it was not unusual to use them for safety for both people and animals during the flood season.

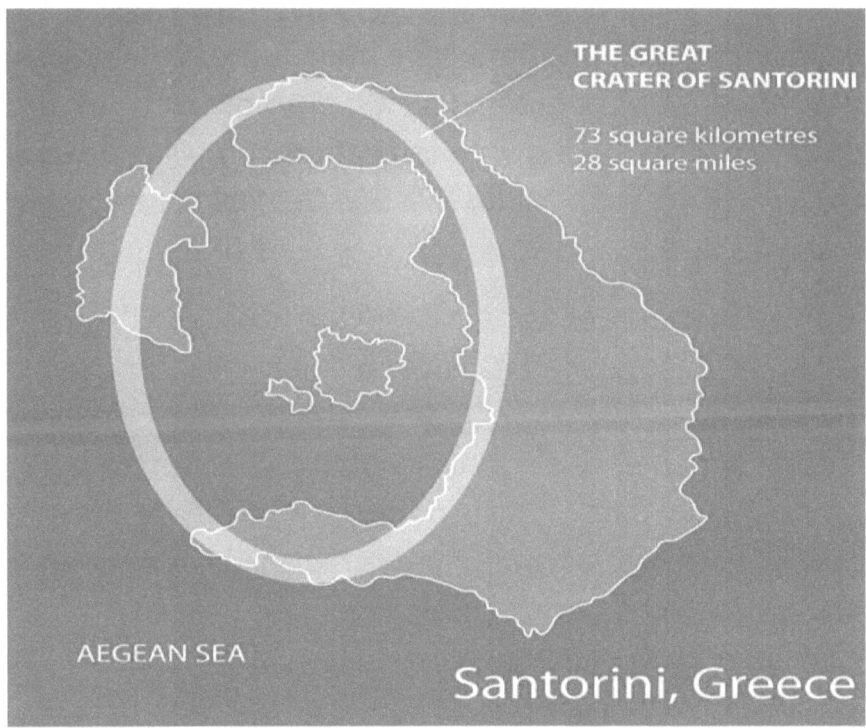

THE GREAT
CRATER OF SANTORINI

73 square kilometres
28 square miles

AEGEAN SEA

Santorini, Greece

Circa the year 1646 BCE (give or take one or two decades) the then sparsely populated World witnessed one of the most earth-staggering phenomenon of the post Neolithic Revolution era. The Aegean island of Thera, now known as Santorini, exploded with a force six times greater than the monstrous eruption of Krakatoa in

Southeast Asia. It was one hundred times more powerful than the Vesuvius eruption at Pompeii and blew out the interior of Santorini forever altering its physiognomy while leaving a vast 73 square kilometer (28 square miles) crater.

The eruption of Krakatoa in Southeast Asia in 1883 CE was heard 3,000 miles or 4,830 km away. It caused the death of over 36,000 people while releasing 20 million tons of sulfur into the atmosphere. It produced a volcanic winter reducing worldwide temperatures by 1.2 degrees Celsius for five years and caused extremely heavy rainfall in Australia. Santorini's explosion was six times greater!

The eruption of Mount Vesuvius was described in a 1956 TIME magazine article as having had the strength of 100,000 times the atom bombs dropped on Hiroshima and Nagasaki. If, as previously notated, Santorini was 100 times greater than Vesuvius, then it would have equated to being ten million times greater than these two atom bombs which were dropped on Japan. Their implementation and delivery effectively brought an abrupt end to Japan's part in WWII.

Both the above analogies involving Krakatoa and Vesuvius strongly emphasize the unbelievable strength with which Santorini exploded. The magnitude of its force was so great that it sent mountainous tsunamis in all directions wreaking havoc on the Aegean islands and Mediterranean shores. Estimates are that the tsunamis were over 250 meters or 800 feet high and that some 36,000 people died as a result. This death count was a staggering number given the relatively sparse population at that point in history.

The significant physical aspect to observe is Santorini's location in the Aegean Sea vis-à-vis the Taurus Mountains rising some 300 kilometers to the east in what is present-day southeastern Turkey. This is the range that feeds water to the mighty Tigris and Euphrates river system which watered ancient Mesopotamia.

The prevailing winds come from the due west in this locale and would have continued to blow the enormous water and tephra saturated clouds towards the Middle East and the Taurus Mountains where they would have settled and produced massive amounts of continuous rainfall. It is highly conceivable that it could have been for forty days and forty nights.

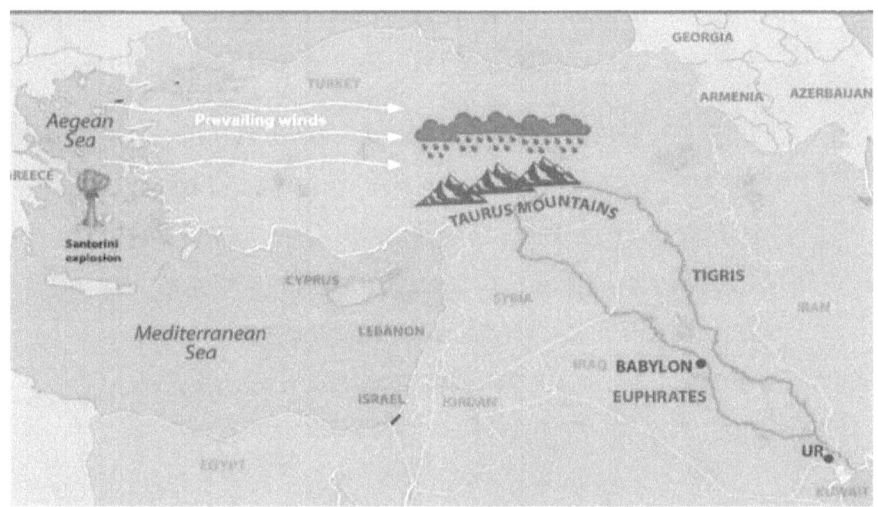

More importantly and in line with the theme of this chapter, gigantic amounts of steam and tephra were thrust into the atmosphere over an extended period. The steam would continue for a number of weeks as the vast 73 sq km (28 sq mi) caldera continued to seethe and ooze magma from a depth of 1.6 km or one mile below sea level. The lava flow into the huge crater left by the blast gushed and steamed for many weeks and eventually formed an island in the middle of the crater.

Besides the occupants of the Ark, there were many witnesses to the Flood (apparently they survived) and they passed down what was observed by word of mouth and from generation to generation. In 1909, Russian-born scholar Rabbi Louis Ginzberg had published his 'The Legend of the Jews', a comprehensive compilation in seven volumes of Aggadah or legends, parables and anecdotes from the Talmud and Jewish lore. With regard to the Flood, he has been quoted with the following in describing what legend had to say regarding the rain that fell during the forty days and nights of the Great Flood:

> *God bade each drop pass through Hell of Gehenna before it fell to earth, and the 'hot rain' scalded the skin of the sinners. The punishment that overtook them was befitting their crimes. As their sensual desires had made them hot, and inflamed them to immoral excesses, so they were chastised by means of heated water.*

What was referred to in Ginzberg's 'Legends' as hot rain may well have been accretionary lapilli. These are small particles that form after a volcanic eruption as moist aggregates in clouds, usually caused by rain that falls through dry eruption clouds.

Further evidence of the Santorini disaster's involvement came from not too distant Egypt with information inscribed on a monument known historically as the 'Tempest Stela' as erected by Pharaoh Ahmose I circa 1550 BCE. The stele has on it a description of a great storm that had occurred accompanied by incessant rain and striking Egypt during this time destroying tombs, temples and pyramids.

The evidence points to the fact that the Santorini cataclysm was the cause of the Great Flood and that Noah and Abraham were alive concurrently at the time it took place. Strong evidence supporting this theory was that both these men were said to have lived together as citizens for a lengthy period (some say 39 years) in the city of Ur in the 1600's BCE and during the time of the explosion.

Noah was purported to have lived 950 years while Abraham 175 years. I am going to go out on a limb with regard to their longevity and suggest that there was poetic license employed in arriving at their respective ages. It appears that exaggeration of the ages of noteworthy people in the records may have started with the Sumerian King List where ancient Mesopotamian kings were reported to have lived thousands of years. (See Chapter III: Messages from Mesopotamia)

According to the Christian Apologetics and Research Ministry, the Bible was written starting around 1445 BCE and completed some 1,500 years later or around 80 CE. If this is true, the writing of the Bible would have begun about 200 years after the Biblical Great Flood as generated by the Santorini cataclysm and 180 years after the deaths of Abraham and Noah.

I believe it is fair to conclude that the Thera/Santorini volcanic cataclysm, having a major effect on climate at the time was the cause of the 40day/40night rainfall that caused the catastrophic Biblical flood.

V
RELIGION AND BUSINESS

THE TEN RICHEST RELIGIOUS ENTITIES IN THE WORLD:

1. The Roman Catholic Church
2. Islam
3. Judaism
4. The Church of Jesus Christ of Latter Day Saints (Mormon)
5. The Church of England (Anglican)
6. Episcopalian
7. Televangelism
8. Protestantism
9. Freemasonry
10. The Church of Scientology

(source: Church and State Press)

Historically, the main source of revenue for religious Institutions has been the contributions by followers.

For Christian institutions, the method has been by way of tithing. The word tithe comes from the Old English teotha which means simply tenth, or the fraction of one's earnings a follower should pay annually to the Church. With most Christian sects, this is a target amount but not a mandatory requirement and access to the parish is not disallowed if it is not met. However, the Mormon Church makes it a prerequisite before allowing entry to temple. This may explain its standing as the fourth wealthiest religious entity while having a comparatively low following of only 16 million people worldwide.

Islam garners its revenue by way of Zakat or a $1/40^{th}$ (2.5%) assessment based on a follower's total wealth (not earnings). Zakat only applies over a minimum amount called Nisab and is voluntary in most Muslim majority countries. However, it is mandatory in nations such as Saudi Arabia and Libya, where the Zakat is collected by the state.

Hindu and Buddhist communities are sustained by a contribution from followers known as Dana. There is no stipulated rate, and any amounts are left to the discretion of the contributor.

The question arises, how much did the economic potential aspect of these religions play in their evolution, or was it just an incidental but very lucrative by-product? Historians seem to overlook the economic factors in the origin of a religion or religious belief system, as evidence is just not available.

Most religions are generally perceived by their followers and most of the public as enormous, impeccable, centuries-old charitable and caring institutions that were inspired by a force greater than man and whose objective is to be beneficial to loyal adherents while representing and preaching morality.

While playing the role of caring for the well-being of and providing services for their parishioners and followers, the monotheistic religions, from inception, have been busy privately, if not secretively, dealing with the more practical aspect of their operation and have always been highly lucrative ventures that have now grown to be mega-powerful institutions.

With regard to the carrying out of the business of religion, the base of the product they are selling is intangible and costs very little to produce, while the revenues can be substantial, depending on how well the product is presented. If Henry David Thoreau's observation that *'the mass of men live lives of quiet desperation'* has meaning and given the credulous nature one may postulate for a good number of we common folk, the product appears not too difficult to sell, resulting in a good source of revenue.

Mainstream groups such as the Catholic, Anglican and Mormon Churches and, of course, Islam, have evolved into economic behemoths so large and spread over so many countries that, when looking at them from the outside and abetted by feeble financial reporting requirements, it is almost impossible to put an exact figure on their staggering net worth. There is reason to believe that only the hierarchy of clerics inside the institution is aware of their real monetary value, and there is a suspicion that prevails that they prefer that not everyone knows.

To give an example of one religious order's size, in 2012, the Economist reported that the collective expenditures of the Catholic Church in the United States alone were $170 billion. By comparison, General Motors, Apple Computers, and Daimler AG generated less revenue worldwide in the same year.

Their source of revenue has been and still is tithes and contributions from parishioners, but, almost more importantly now, the return on investment of their gigantic securities, banking, and commercial real estate portfolios.

The clergy, while maintaining an aura of sanctity, are effectively the salesmen, and the cleric hierarchy, in consort with professional advisers, are the financial managers.

Of course, it didn't start that way, or did it?

At the outset, Judaism and later its offshoot, Christianity were basically local nationalistic (Judaic) belief systems whose framework evolved by way of example and influence of the theocratic empires of Egypt, Assyria and Babylonia all of whom had occupied the Levant at separate times during the preceding centuries as a part of their empires.

The established mode of theocracy at that time for the Fertile Crescent, while unofficial, was for each national or racial group to have its own but similar theistic religion. This, of course, was not planned, but the concept of Fertile Crescent theism was first spawned in that geographic area by early Mesopotamian rulers who had presented themselves as long-living human deities. This is evidenced specifically by historical treasure cuneiform manuscripts, the *Sumerian King List,* and the *Epic of Gilgamesh,* and contrasts dramatically with religions in India and the Far East that developed concurrently but without putting the emphasis on a main God and human half-gods.

While all other religions had been polytheistic, the organizers of Judaism opted for the one-god format.

Judaism and Christianity were being followed by a group of people comprising a few thousand who lived in a small portion of the southern part of the Levant. However, the Roman occupation of Judea and Egypt as a part of its imperial expansion would change that. Although not all historians agree on why the emperor Constantine converted himself and, effectively, the Roman Empire to Christianity, there is evidence that indicates that a substantial number of the officers and troops of the Roman army while being stationed in Judea and Coptic Egypt had become involved with Christianity and that this may have been the deciding factor in the Emperor's decision in the year 312 CE to install it as the official state religion for the whole Roman Empire.

Constantine was an army commander and getting troops to go hard into battle was probably an ongoing major concern. Certainly, providing them with a belief system that featured a heavenly afterlife may have been a key part in his decision to go with Christianity.

Fourth-century historian and bishop Eusebius of Caesarea reported that before the great battle with Western Roman Emperor Maxentius at the Tiber River's Mulvian Bridge, Constantine saw a flaming cross in the sky bearing the words "in this sign thou shalt conquer." Supposedly, this was the event that motivated him to convert to Christianity. Constantine did win the battle, but believing that the sign in the sky even occurred and then was responsible for his winning the battle and subsequent conversion should be regarded as a bit of a stretch.

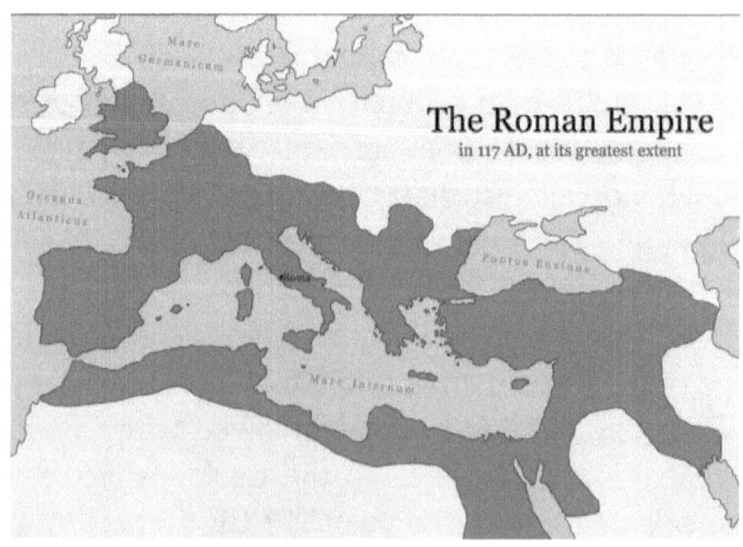

The Roman Empire
in 117 AD, at its greatest extent

In any event, with Constantine's firm endorsement, Christianity received a major boost and went on to become the world's most important mega-religion. With a belief system being backed by the ruling authority of a vast and powerful empire, it then became incumbent on the citizenry to respond and support it which they did. Eventually, structured ministries grew, sects with Roman Catholicism leading the way, developed within the realm and ultimately awe-inspiring cathedrals were built out of the generous revenue stream. This formed part of the let's say "corporate" strategy to maintain the aura of holiness and assisted in retaining and increasing enrolment.

Many financial analysts contend that the monotheistic religions have always been cash generators and this has been the motivating factor for many people, especially males, to become involved in religion as a profession. Considering that there were just a few and mostly arduous professional choices available at the time of formation of these religions, being a priest had to be an attractive and easy way to make a lucrative living, especially if one had a natural way with people and had been gifted as a smooth raconteur. In fact, it was a coveted profession because of the high status it held within society and usually went to those with ties to the ruling hierarchy.

However, history books generally ignore the revenue side of religions and what role it may have played in their evolution and progression. Historians present their analysis with the assumption that a belief system was generated by pious god-fearing individuals who really believed all the stories that formed the foundation for their belief. However, it is a fact that not all were believers and that their façade of belief was more out of necessity.

Of course we will never know what was really in their individual or collective heads but certainly the lucrative nature along with the added political and social power feature of organized religion and the ease with which the general public was and still are willing to accept tales of the supernatural, had to be major considerations by the founders.

This theory has been borne out in more recent times with the creation of religions like Mormonism and Scientology where charismatic men of questionable backgrounds citing dubious occurrences were allowed, without legal recourse, to create very profitable non-taxable belief enterprises. The heavy emphasis in both these religions appears to be, briefly, the cleansing and clearing of one's conscience, something that is appealing to many people.

It is probable that there would have been many more attempts to create new creeds in earlier times had not the established institutions such as the Roman Catholic Church been so powerful and self-protective. The

Protestant movement was met with brutal repression at its outset by Vatican-influenced heresy charges and subsequent executions by burning at the stake.

Religious businesses maintain themselves by finding new followers through proselytizing and by retention of current members by offering them a product that provides satisfaction and relief.

Besides conducting weekly and holiday services, they have founded or supported many charities, established their own schools of higher learning, and occasionally aided by offering relief in some trouble spots in the world. In so doing they basically maintain an aura of unquestionable devotion to the public good.

Certainly, offering atonement and forgiveness are major selling features. Having one's conscience cleansed ultimately, in most cases, at the expense of the injured party, is a major relief to many people. Judaism has Yom Kippur, Christianity has the atonement by way of Messianic human sacrifice while Islam has its Tawbah.

Along with conscience-cleansing, monotheisms also sell rituals such as marriages, bar mitzvahs, baptisms, and funeral services and offer centers where many parishioners may organize their social life and circle of friends through mingling with people who outwardly share the same beliefs.

This type of operation holds another big advantage over all other enterprises in retaining customers in that they are staffed by individuals who are looked upon by many of their followers as holy beings who have a privileged connection to the supernatural power that forms the basis for the faith. As an example, Shiite Muslims believe that their imams were chosen by God to be perfect examples of the faithful. They must be followed as they were appointed by God and are free from sin.

However the real advantage that they hold over other industries, is not having to pay taxes. This provides a broad latitude for administration by their executive and making the establishment of a new and qualifying religion an ideal target for ambitious entrepreneurs. Qualified religions pay no income or real estate taxes. The latter are not assessed although their employees and membership use the expensive infrastructure of a city or town to allow them and their parishioners use and access to and from their facilities.

While there is an emphasis in returning some of their revenues back to charitable causes, the ratio of what is earned and what is paid out in this regard is staggeringly miniscule. The Mormon Church boasts of its generosity yet disburses only 0.7 percent of its annual income for worthy causes. This finding is as a result of a study made by a team from the University of Tampa covering a period of 23 years from 1985 to 2008.

How much does the United States government forgo annually by not taxing religious institutions? This same University of Tampa team, headed by Professor Ryan T. Cragun, calculated that the government loses $71.1 billion annually.

The professor and his students examined U.S. tax laws to estimate the total cost of tax exemptions for religious institutions. The article presenting their findings appears on the website of Council for Secular Humanism, an organization of non theists.

In not paying income taxes there is no stringent requirement to report the real audited financial results for public consumption. Most religious institutions are spread throughout the world and depending on the national territory are required to report certain information with regard to maintaining their tax-exempt status. In most local jurisdictions, there are no global holdings and financial results reporting requirement. There is also no requirement as to legal structure such as incorporation. Therefore there is no legal requirement to produce audited financial statements for financial contributor or parishioner scrutiny.

However, the golden years or I should say centuries of copious cash flow from church operations for the large Christian denominations such as Anglican and Roman Catholic churches are being tested as more transparency is being demanded. Parishioner enrolment is beginning to rapidly dwindle and property maintenance, fixed asset refurbishment and replacement costs are becoming onerous in spite of the eternal tax holiday. Nevertheless, the major players are so deep in real estate and other investment holdings that they should be able to withstand the downward trend for quite a while.

During the 1970's, I was personally involved in a study for a large pension fund which contemplated acquiring, as an investment, a commercial office tower totalling one million square feet located in downtown Montreal. During the negotiations we were told by the seller's legal counsel, in very hushed tones, that the present owner and now vendor was a wholly owned subsidiary of the Vatican. This piece of real estate is still a landmark office building in Montreal and was a part of the Church's huge commercial real estate portfolio. Although we never found out the reason behind the sale of such a gem, there were suspicions that there was a need for cash to pay for certain reparations for the sexual misconduct of some of the clergy.

Of course, if one is to pick an example of a successful private religious enterprise, the Catholic Church is at the head of the list. While Islam with its 1.6 billion faithful would be larger, there is no central authority and most Muslims live in theocracies where religion is a branch or is the government.

I don't begrudge the different religious organizations from earning money. They do provide a service that is important to many people and the majority of the clergy are interested in doing good for all mankind. However, the door is wide open for them to be more forthcoming and transparent in their monetary dealings. The very basis of any religion should be honesty and openness as this is what they preach. Maintaining secrecy on most of their financial dealings and status puts them apart and above their parishioners.

This leaves a condition which is open to a wide variety of abuses even by those with the best intentions. It allows for frivolous spending with little recourse or criticism.

Making religious institutions taxable on income and property, even if the rate is lower than corporations, could be a start to arriving at a reasonable compromise.

VI
RELIGION AND
THE CRIME RATE

Suspicious – To admit a belief merely because it is a custom, but that means to be dishonest, cowardly, lazy! – And so could dishonesty, cowardice and laziness be the preconditions for morality? From Nietzsche's Daybreaks, s.101, R.J. Hollingdale transl.

Does the increasing trend towards secularism around the World also increase immorality? The question has arisen as to whether being religious makes one a more moral person.

The general prevailing view that most people have is that if religious belief is diminished, the effect will be very negative. Crime will soar, violence will increase and society will decay.

However, when one reviews the statistics, it appears that the less a country is religious, the less crime it experiences.

In selecting those countries with a high percentage of irreligious or secular people and comparing them with their crime rate, one can quickly come to the conclusion that non-belief in a deity does not appear to diminish one's moral character, at least when it comes to breaking the law. In fact, these same countries enjoy a significantly lower crime rate than most supposedly predominantly religious nations.

The Crime Index is based on the crime rate per one thousand of the population. The higher the Index, the more crimes are being committed in that country.

The Index is calculated based on the eight crimes that the United States Federal Bureau of Investigation combines to produce its annual Crime Index. These offenses include willful homicide, forcible rape, robbery, burglary, aggravated assault, larceny over $50, motor vehicle theft, and arson.

SECULARISM AND THE CRIME INDEX

The following is a list of the top ten countries in 2021, showing the percentage of the population who claim to be either irreligious or atheist or both, and compares them to their respective Crime Index. Data is supplied by the World Population Review. Polling is by WIN/Gallup International.

The Crime Index average for all countries in the World is 47.86.

COUNTRY	Irreligious	Crime Index
China	90%	31.18
Japan	87%	21.67
Estonia	84%	23.56
Sweden	81%	47.43
Norway	79%	34.62
Czech Rep.	77%	23.40
Hong Kong	74%	20.91
Netherlands	74%	27.15
Israel	70%	30.44
United Kingdom	70%	44.54
AVERAGE	**79%**	**30.49**

It should be noted that the Crime Indices for all ten of the most irreligious countries listed above are below the international average of 47.86 and the total average of 30.49 is significantly lower.

Only Sweden and the United Kingdom are anywhere near the average while still remaining below.

The following are the ten countries with the highest crime rate as indicated by their Crime Index and are compared to their corresponding Irreligious rate.

COUNTRY	Irreligious	Crime Index
Venezuela	12%	84.36
Papua New Guinea	5%	80.04
South Africa	32%	77.29
Afghanistan	9%	76.97
Honduras	23%	76.65
Trinidad and Tobago	13%	72.43
Brazil	16%	68.31
Guyana	3%	68.15
El Salvador	24%	67.84
Syria	2%	67.42
AVERAGE	14%	73.95

All ten countries relative to their irreligiousness, with an average of 14% reflect a Crime Index average of 73.95, which is significantly higher than the world average of 47.86. What both analyses show is clearly obvious: the less religious the country, the lower the crime rate.

SECULARISM AND THE GLOBAL PEACE INDEX

The other index that works statistically in favor of the less religious is the Global Peace Index (GPI). It indicates clearly that the more peaceful nations are the ones with the least religious population, while the more warlike countries are the most religious.

The GPI is a composite index measuring the peacefulness of countries made up of 23 quantitative and qualitative indicators, each measured on a scale of 1 to 5. The lower the score, the more peaceful the country.

The following are the ten most peaceful countries in the World:

COUNTRY	Irreligious	GPI
Iceland	42%	1.08
New Zealand	48%	1.20
Portugal	28%	1.25
Austria	45%	1.28
Denmark	80%	1.28
Canada	57%	1.30
Singapore	30%	1.32

Czech Rep.	75%	1.34
Japan	87%	1.36
Switzerland	57%	1.37
AVERAGE	**55%**	**1.28**

According to Vision of Humanity, a nonprofit organization that issues an annual Global Peace Index, each of the ten safest and most peaceful nations in the World is also among the most secular and least god-believing. Conversely, most of the least peaceful and unsafe nations are extremely religious. Examples of eleven larger countries with a high GPI and their related irreligious population:

COUNTRY	Irreligious	GPI
China	90%	2.22
Brazil	16%	2.27
United States	39%	2.40
Iran	20%	2.54
India	5%	2.61
Venezuela	12%	2.67
Pakistan	6%	2.97
Russia	30%	3.09
Syria	2%	3.41
Iraq	34%	3.57
Afghanistan	9%	3.70
AVERAGE	**24%**	**2.86**

Only China with its irreligious population at 90% somewhat distorts the final average. However, the pattern is quite discernible with the remaining ten countries all of which indicate an irreligious rate well below 40%.

CONCLUSION

The use of the Crime Index and Global Peace Index as the ultimate tools for measuring morality has certain limitations. However, these indices appear to be the best measurements available and are tangibly useable to arrive at an understandable statistical conclusion. It is imperfect to conclude that secularism, alone, results in good moral behavior or that religiosity is the cause of social misbehavior. There are other contributing factors such as economics, culture, history, geography, and politics that also have an influence.

However, the evidence is quite clear that the presence of an increased movement toward secularism does not pose the threat that many rightwing conservatives claim it does. The evidence displayed is so overwhelming that a strong majority would be justified in concluding that most societies if they wanted to be more peaceful and have a lower crime rate, would be better off without religion.

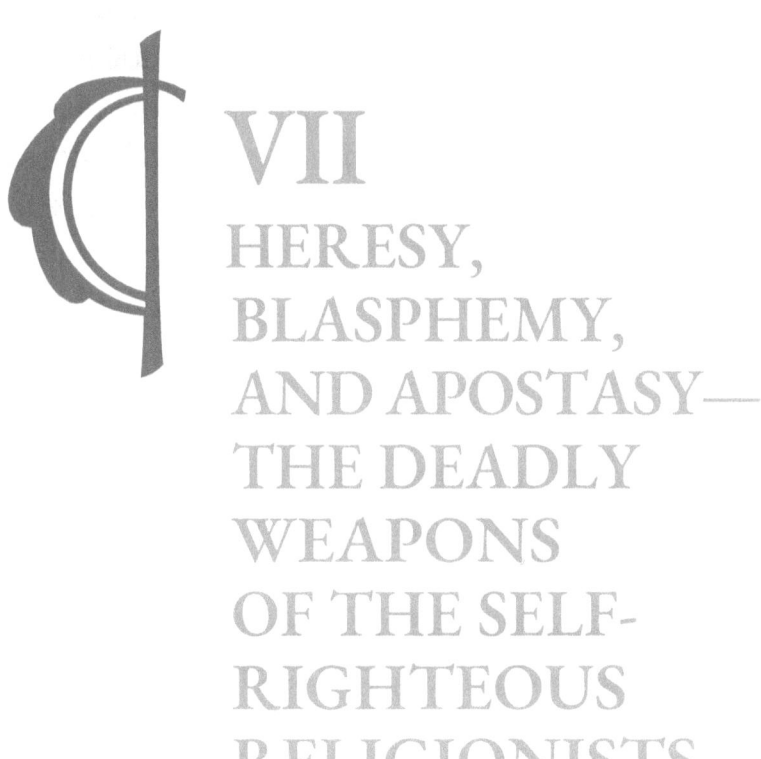

VII
HERESY, BLASPHEMY, AND APOSTASY— THE DEADLY WEAPONS OF THE SELF-RIGHTEOUS RELIGIONISTS

Christianity and Islam as religions are both strong financially and in their number of followers. One way they so evolved was by fastidiously, if not fiercely, protecting their belief systems, their scriptures and the people who support and preach them.

Both religions have had built, at great expense over the ages millions of sometimes very imposing houses of worship to attract, service and maintain their following. Christianity has over twenty million churches while Islam is approaching four million mosques. From a business standpoint, this represents an enormous investment that requires protection. The best way to protect one's revenue stream is to ensure that membership and attendance remain stable and hopefully grow.

What they are selling is based on stories from the past involving humans encountering never-seen and never- to-be-seen supernatural deities, all of which requires a great deal of faith to believe. American comedian, actor and political commentator, Bill Maher, when talking about the clergy and religious leaders has said on occasion: "They're selling air". Well, it's probably a little thicker than air but not by much.

The doctrines and tenets of the theistic religions require that their followers believe stories from the past that are heavily based on the paranormal. Figures such as God, Zeus, the Holy Spirit, Allah, Yahweh, Satan, holy angels and jinn have never been seen except by a chosen few a long time ago and only as reported by the gospels. With no factual evidence of their existence, it is difficult to believe that they do exist unless there is an unquestioning faith in the scriptures and those who preach them.

If one is to believe the power attributed to these deities, then there have been many occasions where their presence should have occurred. As examples, the horror of the Holocaust, the Armenian genocide and two bloody World Wars were met with no-shows and silence from the deities with no indication that these all-powerful gods cared or could do anything about them.

HERESY

The Medieval Church which was the Catholic Church before the Protestant Reformation around 1500 CE held great power in the past. Today, Islam, as it functions in certain Muslim theocracies wields a similar authority.

Heresy can be defined as a belief or action at odds with what is accepted, especially when the behavior is contrary to religious belief or doctrine.

Today, heresy, when it occurs and relates to ecumenical doctrine is frowned upon by the Catholic Church but little is or can be done to legally punish the apparent detractor. This was not the case in the Middle Ages (476 to 1500 CE) when the Medieval Catholic Church wielded incredible power. The Church had the authority to tax and its laws had to be obeyed. It was to be feared and its influence spread into every facet of society as it established a monopoly over the spiritual life of Europeans.

The prime example of religious zealotry gone totally mad was the establishment by the Catholic Church in the twelfth century of the Inquisition. It was comprised of a council of senior priests in various jurisdictions across Europe who would search out heretics and bring them to justice as decided by the Church. Its main objective was to combat heresy by severely punishing the abusers.

Those who were considered heretics and who did not recant were handed over to the civil authorities who would administer various forms of severe punishment. The most notorious was the execution by being burned alive at the stake.

The Inquisition was to last for hundreds of years and was responsible for taking the lives of tens of thousands of innocent people. I say innocent because heresy is not a crime under secular law. However, it was looked upon as a serious crime against the Church who dictated the law at that time.

There is nothing in the Bible that says that heretics should be punished with death. This was the contrivance of the Church in order to maintain control over its followers through the use of coercion. The threat of being burned alive was certainly a deterrent to those who wished to question or leave the Church of whom there was most likely a sizeable number.

One of the more famous victims of the Inquisition was astronomer, physicist and engineer, Galileo Galilei, commonly known by his first name only. Having made telescopic probes into the Universe and particularly our Solar System, Galileo was to conclude that the Earth revolved around the Sun which is a condition known as heliocentrism. His conclusion was in agreement with that of Polish astronomer, Nicolaus Copernicus who theorized a century earlier that the Sun was the centre of the Universe.

In 1632, Galileo published his findings and opinion in his very popular *Dialogue Concerning the Two Chief World Systems* which defended heliocentrism. This caused great consternation within the Church which preached that the Earth was the centre of the Universe and that the Sun revolved around it. In 1633, Galileo was charged with and found guilty of being "vehemently suspect of heresy" by the Roman Inquisition and sentenced to life imprisonment. The sentence was later commuted to house arrest under which he lived until his death in 1642.

The two more famous factions, the Roman and Spanish Inquisitions, finally were disbanded in 1834 after almost four hundred years of on and off terrorizing people. Although it took many centuries, the Church finally realized it had gone too far and had strayed badly from the tenets of Christianity. With regard to Galileo, it was not until 1992 that the Vatican apologized for his condemnation admitting that it was a mistake.

While the Catholic Church had dramatically reduced the punishment for heretics, it still maintained their classification as being very negative. The breakaway Protestant movement was branded as heretical even though it was Christian.

BLASPHEMY AND APOSTASY

Blasphemy is defined as an insult that shows disrespect, contempt or lack of reverence regarding a deity, a sacred object or a religious belief. Apostasy is the act of renunciation or disaffiliation of a religious or political belief. By rejecting one's faith may also be considered as committing blasphemy in the eyes of certain religious law interpreters.

Blasphemy laws have been on the books of many countries for many centuries although not being enforced in many cases. However, a number of democratic countries including Canada, France and the United Kingdom have taken action to repeal such laws as they take away the citizen's right to criticize under freedom of speech. The emphasis is on the word 'criticize' which means that it should not be done in an insulting manner so as to avoid sanctions. Certain large countries are without blasphemy laws such as the United States, China and Argentina.

However, there are eight nations that do have blasphemy laws for which the penalty is death! In order of the largest population first, they include: Nigeria,

Pakistan, Iran, Afghanistan, Somalia, Mauritania, Saudi Arabia and Brunei. Large countries with blasphemy laws where the punishment is imprisonment are: India, Indonesia, Bangladesh and Russia.

With regard to the countries with death penalties, all are 99% Muslim except Nigeria which is split 50/50 between Christian and Muslim.

Take note that there is no category in these statistics for secularists. According to the Pew Research Center global study in 2012 of 230 countries, 16% of the World's population is not affiliated with any religion. Yet we see that the death penalty countries are almost fully booked at 99% with no dissidents. This means that the death threat is working in favor of the Mosque. One can only guess at the number of people who wish to leave Islam but are afraid for their lives.

SALMAN RUSHDIE

Probably the most notable use of the blasphemy clause came in 1989 when the Ayatollah Khomeini, the leader of the Iranian Revolution and founder of the Islamic Republic of Iran declared a death *fatwa* against British author, Salman Rushdie.

Rushdie was born in 1947 to a Muslim family in India. He was educated in Bombay and Warwickshire, England and went into advertising in London. He has described himself as a "secular human being" who does not believe in the supernatural. He became a successful author with three books to his credit before he wrote the fateful book, *The Satanic Verses*, the subject of the *fatwa*. The following is what was announced by the Ayatollah on Tehran radio on February 14, 1989:

> *In the name of Him, the Highest. There is only one God, to whom we shall all return.*
>
> *I inform all zealous Muslims of the World that the author of the book entitled 'The Satanic Verses' which has been compiled, printed and published in opposition to Islam, the Prophet and the Qur'an and all those involved in its publication who were aware of its content, are sentenced to death.*
>
> *I call all zealous Muslims to execute them quickly, wherever they may be found, so that no one else will dare to insult the Muslim sanctities. God willing, whoever is killed on this path is a martyr.*
>
> *In addition, anyone who has access to the author of this book but does not possess the power to execute him should report him to the people so that he may be punished for his actions.*
>
> *May peace and the mercy of God and His Blessings be with you.*

An additional bounty was also offered to the successful assassin. If he was Iranian, 200 million Iranian riyals (about $160,000) and for a non-Iranian, $1,000,000.

Rushdie first heard the news from the BBC World Service. He soon went into hiding under the protection of the British Police and would spend the next decade and more under police protection and in secrecy.

What is evident by the past abhorrent actions of the Medieval Church and by present-day Islam's behavior as practiced in some Muslim countries that require the death penalty to retain followers could be interpreted as a major weakness in the backbone of their religion.

I have great respect for the people of Islam but feel, that excess zealotry and the demeaning of infidels in the scriptures detracts from the objective of arriving at a harmonious and peaceful World.

VIII
RELIGION AND THE AFTERLIFE

Major Religious Classifications as of 2020	Followers
Christianity	2.382 billion
Islam	1.907 billion
Secular	1.193 billion
Hindu	1.161 billion
Buddhism	.506 billion
Others (15)	.641 billion
Total	**7.790 billion**

The major religions all offer varying forms of seraphic afterlife in what most identify as 'Heaven'. Each has its particular slant, essentially presenting after one's death, an ethereal, eternal, and final stage to one's existence.

The negative side, which is known familiarly as 'Hell' is presented in various fashions and names but is well known to involve a great deal of fire and eternal suffering.

In both cases, it is clear that Heaven and Hell appear to be creations of man. They are and have been used as tools, on one hand to soften the fear and impact of death, and on the other hand, to threaten severe punishment to those who wish to disbelieve in the deity or transgress against the social order.

Evidence that man believed in the afterlife surfaced many millennia before formal religions were established. Anthropologists have discovered burial sites dating back as far as 30,000 BCE that show the remains of Homo sapiens buried along with food, weapons and personal artifacts. Even the Neanderthals, dating back to 100,000 BCE, were found to have buried their dead with food, stone implements, and decorative shells and bones.

By including such a collection of items with the demised person's body, it appears that the mourners were attempting to equip a beloved who had passed on with the supplies that would assist in the transition to the spiritual world after death.

It is not surprising that an advanced species of mammal, as are Homo sapiens and as were Neanderthals (before they became extinct), would propagate the existence of a heavenly afterlife. It appears to be an attempt to mitigate the anxiety and natural fear of dying that most humans have by assuring those still living that their existence is not over when they die. In addition, the death of loved ones is less painful if one truly believes they have gone to a better place.

Belief in a heavenly afterlife has been a major implement for the larger religions mainly in bringing comfort to their followers before one's death or when death of another arrives in their midst.

Belief in the existence of a frightful place such as Hell to where one would have to go after death acts as a deterrent to those who are not believers in the Faith or wish to behave badly.

The assumed need for a place like Hell probably evolved during the Neolithic Revolution. As described in Chapter II, the Neolithic started about 12,000 years ago, during which the world population evolved a new but ultimately very competitive pattern of behavior. The chaos that followed gave cause for those responsible for social order to create a Hell. Their aim was to alleviate the lawlessness and strife prompted by the new but yet unrefined economic condition.

There is agreement that the threat of going to Hell may well act as a deterrent against misconduct. However, there are many who believe that it is more important to live a life without the need for false facades and assistance from the supernatural. Refer to Chapter VI about the crime rate being lower for a secular society than a religious one.

TOO MANY PEOPLE IN BOTH HEAVEN AND HELL?

An important issue that casts doubt on their existence is the incredible number of souls presently located in both Heaven and Hell.

This prompted an exercise to attempt to determine just how many dead people have been directed to the fiery confines of Hell and the same question as to how many went through the Gates of Heaven since the beginning of the existence of man.

In order to arrive at a rough estimate, the number of people who are presently in prison in the entire World, as supplied by the National Institute of Corrections, has been taken. This number, which amounts to 10,350,000 prisoners, is divided by the present population of the World, or 8 billion people. The result is a percentage of 0.13%. The assumption has been made that those people presently in prison would have a difficult time reaching heaven. This ratio is conservative, as there are still many people who are roaming about freely who should not be allowed in Heaven according to the rules reported in the scriptures. The Population Research Bureau estimates that there have been 117 billion people ever born to this world; fewer the 8 billion means that 109 billion people have died. Since the year 1 CE or the birth of Christ, there have been 54 billion people who have died, of whom 70 million would have gone to Hell and 53.93 billion would have gone to Heaven, calculated by using the prisoners' percentage.

The numbers would be about double if one used the all-time population figures starting 190,000 years ago.

Bear in mind, these numbers do not diminish over time as the term of one's sentence to Heaven or Hell has been reported as, in most cases, an eternity.

One can only imagine the difficulty of administering seventy million people in Hell. Remember that this does not include secularists who didn't qualify to go to heaven, which would number in the billions. There must be a very large army of assistant Satans to administer the pain.

At the other level, the billions of souls of people writhing and roaming about in Heaven must make it one 'helluva' place. (I couldn't resist the opportunity) But seriously, is it possible that such a vast number of individuals could be gathered in one place and one could still call it Heaven?

I think that having a heaven to go to is a wonderful thing, but is it realistic to think that it exists? With the billions of souls flashing about, to me, it appears more like a living disaster.

Even further, there is a major question as to unbelievers and their destination after death. Presently, there are almost 1.2 billion Secularists in the World. These are nonreligious people and would include atheists, agnostics, and infidels.

The Pope has recently confirmed that all atheists go to Hell. Add the number of infidels as referred to by Islamists, and one could easily end up with an easy billion more having gone or who are going to Hell.

In any event, the numbers for both locales are staggering and might bring some believers to question the practical validity of the existence of an afterlife.

Despite these overwhelming numbers in this little experiment, a large majority of people continue to believe in Heaven and Hell. A poll taken recently by the Pew Research Center indicates that 73% of Americans believe in Heaven and 62% believe in Hell.

There are positives to these beliefs. One must agree that believing in Heaven does offer a great deal of comfort and hope to many people. A belief in Hell could give cause to those who wish to harm to think twice before acting.

The debate between the religious and nonreligious people regarding the existence of an Afterlife will probably continue without being resolved.

EPILOGUE

Writing critically about religion has proven in history to be a somewhat dangerous game.

Previous authors before me who have been negative on religion, such as Sam Harris and Richard Dawkins, have been known to have received hate mail and death threats. Even more clearly defined was the public proclamation by the Ayatollah Khomeini offering a substantial reward to those who would take the life of author Salman Rushdie for his part in writing the 'Satanic Verses.'

My dissatisfaction with parts of the Islamic texts is not a criticism of the people of Islam. It is meant more to draw attention to certain statements in the scriptures, which can stir up hatred toward nonbelievers of the Islamic faith and which I believe have caused and will continue to cause serious problems.

I can only imagine how much greater internationally Islam, which its ardent followers proudly tout as the 'Religion of Peace', would become if the vitriol expressed towards infidels in the Qur'an and Hadith was somehow diluted.

I am confident in the knowledge that the administrators of the religions of Christianity, Judaism, and Islam are aware of the controversial content in their respective scriptures but find making alterations to be, perhaps, too onerous or even impossible. This is why, in Chapter II, it is proposed that a 'Holy Codicil' be employed to clarify the meanings of the less-than-holy declarations in the scriptures without disturbing the original text.

I firmly declare that I do have respect for the religions in question, as I believe they are responsible for many great traditions that have made the lives of many of their followers more comfortable and fulfilled over many centuries.

However, it is time that civilization and its religions mature to a point where interreligious competitions pose no threat to one another and that religions pose no threat to human life.

Let's try to make each and every religion a Religion of Peace for all people.

www.ingramcontent.com/pod-product-compliance
Lightning Source LLC
Chambersburg PA
CBHW021654120626
46545CB00002B/863